FACT CAT

EDITH CAVELL

Izzi Howell

WAYLAND
www.waylandbooks.co.uk

FACT CAT

Get your paws on this fantastic new mega-series from Wayland!

Join our Fact Cat on a journey of fun learning about every subject under the sun!

First published in Great Britain in 2016 by Wayland
Copyright © Wayland 2016

ISBN: 978 0 7502 9772 1
Dewey Number: 940.4'8641'092-dc23
10 9 8 7 6 5 4 3 2 1

MIX
Paper from responsible sources
FSC® C104740

Wayland
An imprint of Hachette Children's Group
Part of Hodder & Stoughton
Carmelite House
50 Victoria Embankment
London EC4Y 0DZ

An Hachette UK Company
www.hachette.co.uk
www.hachettechildrens.co.uk

A catalogue for this title is available from the British Library
Printed and bound in China

Produced for Wayland by
White-Thomson Publishing Ltd
www.wtpub.co.uk

Editor: Izzi Howell
Design: Rocket Design (East Anglia) Ltd
Fact Cat illustrations: Shutterstock/Julien Troneur
Front cover illustration by Wesley Lowe
Consultant: Kate Ruttle

Picture and illustration credits:
Alamy: Chronicle 9, 16 and 19, John Frost Newspapers 17 and 18; Corbis: Hulton-Deutsch Collection 7 and 15, Ton Koene/Visuals Unlimited 21; iStock: duncan1890 6; Shutterstock: Everett Historical 4, 11, 12 and 14, dovla982 5t, chippix 8, BasPhoto 20; Stefan Chabluk: 10; Wellcome Library, London: title page, 5b and 13.

Every effort has been made to clear copyright. Should there be any inadvertent omission, please apply to the publisher for rectification.

The author, Izzi Howell, is a writer and editor specialising in children's educational publishing.

The consultant, Kate Ruttle, is a literacy expert and SENCO, and teaches in Suffolk.

FACT CAT FACT

...is a question for you to answer on most spreads in this book. You can check your answers on page 24.

CONTENTS

WHO WAS EDITH CAVELL?

At the beginning of the 20th **century**, there was a war in Europe. This war is known as the First World War.

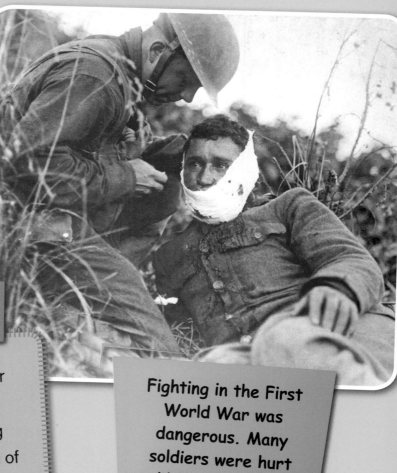

FACT CAT FACT

When the First World War started in 1914, people thought that the fighting would be over by the end of the year. In which year did the First World War finish?

Fighting in the First World War was dangerous. Many soldiers were hurt and killed by **weapons** and **bombs**.

Edith Cavell was a nurse who worked in Belgium during the First World War. She worked in a hospital and helped soldiers **escape** from the war to a safer place.

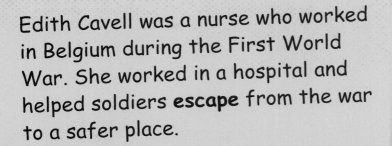

Belgium

Edith Cavell saved the lives of many soldiers in the First World War.

EARLY LIFE

Edith Cavell was born in England in 1865. When she was 16, she left her family home to go to **boarding school**.

After she finished school, Edith Cavell worked as a **governess** in Belgium. Which Belgian city did she work in?

FACT CAT FACT

When Edith was working as a governess, she learned how to speak French because people in some parts of Belgium speak French as their main language.

After helping her father **recover** from an illness, Edith decided to become a nurse. She finished her **training** in 1898, and started work as a nurse in a hospital in London.

Edith Cavell visited her **patients** after they left hospital to make sure that they were getting better.

HOSPITALS AND NURSES

In the early 20th century, people got ill more often than they do today. It was hard for hospitals to treat sick people, because many medicines hadn't been discovered yet.

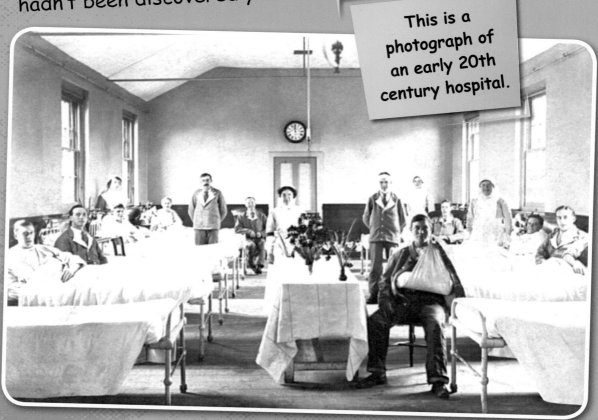

This is a photograph of an early 20th century hospital.

In the past, nurses were always women. They wore white aprons and headbands as part of their uniform.

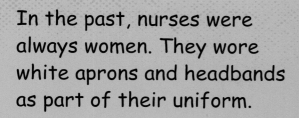

In 1907, Cavell moved back to Belgium to be in charge of a team of nurses. This photo shows Cavell with all the nurses that worked at the hospital.

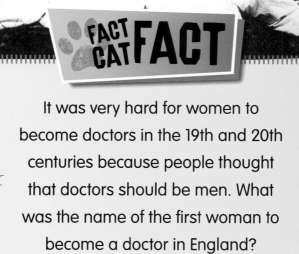

FACT CAT FACT

It was very hard for women to become doctors in the 19th and 20th centuries because people thought that doctors should be men. What was the name of the first woman to become a doctor in England?

THE FIRST WORLD WAR BEGINS

At the beginning of the First World War, Britain, France and Russia fought against Germany and **Austria-Hungary**. Later, more countries joined in.

This map shows the two sides that fought against each other in the beginning of the First World War.

BRITAIN

NETHERLANDS

BELGIUM   GERMANY

RUSSIA

FRANCE

AUSTRIA-HUNGARY

Some countries, such as Belgium, didn't support either side of the war. However, many battles were fought in the countryside of Belgium.

Soldiers lived in **trenches** dug in the **battlefields.** They climbed out of the trenches to fight each other.

FACT CAT FACT

First World War battles were also fought in Russia, Italy and the Middle East. How many countries took part in the First World War?

BACK TO BELGIUM

Edith Cavell was on holiday in England when the First World War started. She went back to Belgium because she wanted to help injured soldiers.

Many injured soldiers were taken from the Belgian battlefields to the hospital where Edith Cavell worked.

Even though Cavell was British, she helped soldiers from both sides of the war. Some British people were angry that Cavell was helping German soldiers, because Germany was Britain's enemy in the war.

Cavell knew that hospitals in Belgium needed good nurses. She said, 'At a time like this, I am needed more than ever.'

FACT CAT FACT

Edith Cavell believed that nurses should take care of all patients, no matter which country they came from.

HELPING SOLDIERS

Soon after the beginning of the First World War, Germany took control of Belgium. It became dangerous for British people to be there, but Edith Cavell didn't leave because she wanted to carry on helping soldiers.

The Germans used **zeppelins** to drop bombs on the cities where their enemies lived.

The Germans wouldn't let the British and French patients in Edith Cavell's hospital leave Belgium. Cavell helped the soldiers escape to the Netherlands, a nearby country where they would be safe.

FACT CAT FACT

Edith Cavell helped nearly 200 men escape from Belgium.

Cavell helped the soldiers get **fake IDs** so that they could go across the **border** between Belgium and the Netherlands. Which other countries share a border with Belgium?

CAVELL'S ARREST

In August 1915, the German police found out that Edith Cavell was helping British soldiers to escape out of Belgium. She was **arrested** and taken to prison.

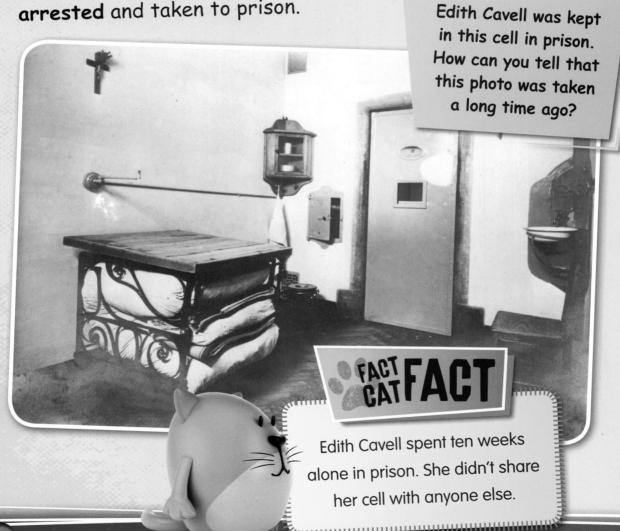

Edith Cavell was kept in this cell in prison. How can you tell that this photo was taken a long time ago?

FACT CAT FACT

Edith Cavell spent ten weeks alone in prison. She didn't share her cell with anyone else.

Cavell told the police the truth about what she had done. The German police decided that they would shoot Edith Cavell as a punishment for helping the soldiers escape.

The German police took Cavell from her cell to an army building in Brussels, where they shot enemy prisoners.

A SAD DAY

Some countries tried to **persuade** the Germans to **forgive** Edith Cavell, but they did not change their mind. Edith Cavell was shot and killed by German soldiers on 12 October 1915.

Edith Cavell's death was on the front page of British newspapers. What does the word 'martyred' in the headline mean?

THE DAILY MIRROR, Friday, October 22, 1915.

TRAGIC STORY OF MISS CAVELL'S HEROIC DEATH

The Daily Mirror

CERTIFIED CIRCULATION LARGER THAN ANY OTHER PICTURE PAPER IN THE WORLD

No. 3,743   Registered at the G.P.O. as a Newspaper.   FRIDAY, OCTOBER 22, 1915.   One Halfpenny.

HAPPY TO DIE FOR HER COUNTRY: HOW MISS CAVELL, THE BRITISH NURSE, WAS MARTYRED BY THE GERMANS.

Mr. Brand Whitlock, the American Minister in Belgium, who left no stone unturned to prevent the infliction of the death penalty. Mr. Whitlock is well known as a novelist in the United States.

The Marquis Villalobar, the Spanish Minister in Belgium, who, with Mr. Whitlock, tried to save Miss Cavell's life.

Miss Cavell in nurse's uniform. She was accused of harbouring Allied soldiers. There was no charge of espionage.

Miss Cavell, who was known as "the Florence Nightingale of Brussels."

To-day the nation's heart will be stirred by the publication of the true story of Miss Edith Cavell, the British nurse, who was executed by the Germans. Every effort to save her was made by Mr. Brand Whitlock and the Marquis Villalobar. At the end Miss Cavell said: "I am happy to die for my country." In response to the appeals of readers, *The Daily Mirror* is organising a Cavell Memorial Fund to perpetuate this heroic woman's memory.

Cavell's body was taken back to England. Her coffin was carried to **Westminster Abbey** in a **procession** through London. Later, she was buried in the city of Norwich.

Many people came to see Edith Cavell's funeral at Westminster Abbey.

REMEMBERING EDITH CAVELL

Today, we remember Edith Cavell for saving the lives of many people. She helped her patients as much as she could, even when it was difficult and dangerous.

There are monuments to Edith Cavell in countries throughout the world. This one is in London.

Although we have better medicines today, it's still hard work being a nurse. Like Edith Cavell, some nurses travel to dangerous places to help people who have been hurt in wars.

Today, both men and women can be nurses. This nurse is helping a patient in the Central African Republic, in Africa.

FACT CAT FACT

In 1917, a **charity** was set up to remember Edith Cavell and help other nurses in the UK. What is the name of this charity?

QUIZ Try to answer the questions below. Look back through the book to help you. Check your answers on page 24.

1 When did the First World War start?

a) 1890

b) 1904

c) 1914

2 Edith Cavell worked as a governess after she finished school. True or not true?

a) true

b) not true

3 Where did Edith Cavell work as a nurse during the First World War?

a) Belgium

b) France

c) Germany

4 Edith Cavell only helped British soldiers. True or not true?

a) true

b) not true

5 How many men escaped from Belgium with Edith Cavell's help?

a) 20

b) 200

c) 2000

6 Edith Cavell's funeral took place in Britain. True or not true?

a) true

b) not true

GLOSSARY

arrest to be taken by the police and asked questions about a crime

Austria-Hungary In the past, this was an empire ruled by one person, but today it is divided into many countries, such as Austria, Hungary and the Czech Republic.

battlefield a place where a battle is fought

boarding school a school where students live and study

bomb a weapon that will explode

border the line that separates two countries

century a period of 100 years. The 20th century refers to dates between 1900 and 1999.

charity an organisation that gives money, food or help to people that need it

escape to get away from a place because it is not safe

fake describes something that isn't real, but looks real

forgive to decide not to be angry with someone for what they have done

governess a woman whose job it is to teach children in their home. In the past, there were many governesses, but there aren't many today.

ID a document with information such as your name and your photo

patient someone who is being treated by a doctor or a nurse

persuade to try to make someone do something by talking to them about it

procession a line of people that moves together slowly as part of an event

recover to become healthy again after an illness

training the time during which you learn the skills that you need to do a job

trench a long narrow hole dug in the ground for soldiers

weapon an object used to hurt or kill someone

Westminster Abbey a large important church in London

zeppelin a large aircraft without wings that floats in the sky

INDEX

ANSWERS

Pages 4–21

page 4: 1918

page 6: Brussels

page 9: Elizabeth Garrett Anderson

page 11: 32 countries

page 15: France, Germany and Luxembourg

page 16: Because it is in black and white.

page 18: It means that Edith Cavell died for what she believed in – helping hurt people.

page 21: Cavell Nurses' Trust

Quiz answers

1 c - 1914
2 true
3 a - Belgium
4 not true – she helped soldiers from both sides.
5 b - 200
6 true

OTHER TITLES IN THE FACT CAT SERIES...

WAYLAND
www.waylandbooks.co.uk